D0339057

best
easy
day hikes

Joshua Tree

Bill Cunningham
Polly Burke

FALCON GUIDES ®

GUILFORD, CONNECTICUT
HELENA, MONTANA
AN IMPRINT OF THE GLOBE PEQUOT PRESS

FALCONGUIDES®

Cover photo by Larry Carver.

Cataloging-in-Publication Data is on record at the Library of Congress.

ISBN 978-1-56044-978-2

Manufactured in the United States of America
First Edition/Third Printing

Contents

Southwest Region

Northwest Region

Dedication

To the thousands of citizens of California and elsewhere, past and present, who laid the groundwork for protection of a large portion of the California desert, to those who helped secure passage of the California Desert Protection Act, and to the dedicated state and federal park rangers and naturalists charged with the stewardship of California's irreplaceable desert wilderness.

Map Legend

Interstate Highway/Freeway	(00)	City		⊞ or ○
US Highway	(00)	Campground		▲
State or Other Principal Road	(00) (000)	Picnic Area		⊼
		Building		■
Park Route	(00)	Peak		9,782 ft.
Interstate Highway	⟹	Elevation		9,782 ft. ✕
Paved Road	⟹	River/Creek		⌣
Gravel Road	⟹	Spring		⟲
Unimproved Road	====⟹	Pass		)(
Trailhead	○	Mine Site		⚒
Parking Area	Ⓟ	Sand Dunes		
Main Trail/Route	••—••—••	Overlook		◨
Main Trail/Route on Road		Forest/Park Boundary		⌐ ⌐|_⌐
Alternate/Secondary Trail/Route	—••—•^•—••	State/International Border		
Alternate/Secondary Trail/Route on Road				
One Way Road	One Way	Map Orientation		N ▲
Road Junction	☐	Scale		0 0.5 1 Miles

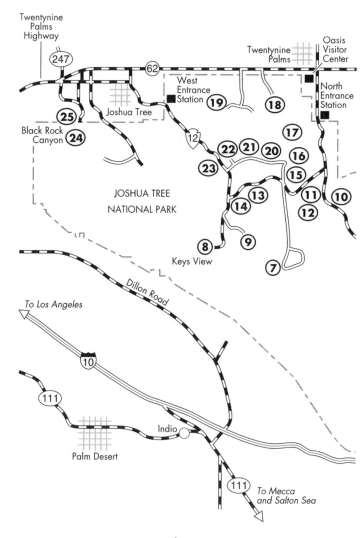

Overview Map of Joshua Tree

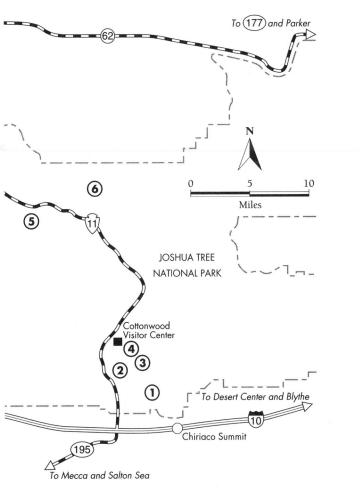

Ranking the Hikes

The following list ranks the hikes in this book from easiest to hardest.

Introduction

Best Easy Day Hikes Joshua Tree is a shortened and updated version of the Joshua Tree National Park section of *Hiking California's Desert Parks.* This compact guidebook features easily accessible hikes that appeal to the full spectrum of visitors—from kids to their grandparents. These 25 hikes sample the best that Joshua Tree has to offer for the casual hiker.

Straddling the transition between the Mojave and Colorado Deserts and containing vast mounds of enchanting granite rock formations, Joshua Tree National Park is a refuge of wild open space close to Los Angeles and next door to sprawling desert communities.

Joshua Tree was upgraded from national monument to national park by the 1994 California Desert Protection Act, and was enlarged from 559,995 acres to 794,000 acres. The 1994 Act also increased wilderness designation to 630,800 acres—70 percent of the park. Mountain ranges define the park's boundaries and dominate its interior. The best known geologic feature in Joshua Tree is its ethereal landscape of gargantuan monzogranite boulders, domes, and peaks, formed by more than 180 million years of uplifting and erosion.

Hiking in the park quickly reveals contrasts between Colorado and Mojave Desert vegetation. Below 3,000 feet, the Colorado Desert encompasses Pinto Basin and other expanses in the east end of the park. The desert is lower, drier, and hotter with creosote, ocotillo, sagebrush, and cholla. The higher, moister Mojave Desert is the domain of Joshua tree forests in the western half of the park. Forests of pinyon-juniper mixed with manzanita adorn mountain slopes, with smoke trees and mesquite in the washes. Joshua trees, namesake of the park, are shallow rooted and slow growing, taking hundreds of years to reach a mature height of 30 feet.

Five desert oases mark the rare occurrence of both water and concentrated wildlife. Most wildlife is nocturnal and usually invisible to the human eye. Coyotes are common, but are only one of 350 vertebrate species that range from ubiquitous mice and wood rats to desert tortoise that are listed as threatened under the Endangered Species Act. Twenty species of snakes and 14 kinds of lizards slither and dart across the desert floor, primarily at night. Equally exciting is the array of birds at Joshua Tree, with more than 230 species on the checklist.

Most of the hikes in *Best Easy Day Hikes Joshua Tree* are short—less than 4 miles round trip and with less than 800 feet of elevation change. More than half the hikes are ideal for families with small children. Two of the hikes, Cap Rock and Keys View Loop, are barrier free and wheelchair accessible. All of the trailheads are reachable by passenger car, and most have a paved road leading to them. All of the best easy day hikes are situated in the western half of the park, which is served by paved highways.

To provide a geographic reference, hikes 1 through 14 are located in the southwest region of the park, as defined by the area south of the junction of Park Routes 11 and 12 and from there south of the area bounded by PR 12 and the Keys View Road. Hikes 15 through 25 are in the northwest corner of the park, north of the highway between the junctions of PR 11 and 12 and of PR 12 with the Keys View Road and from there straight west to the park boundary.

—*Bill Cunningham & Polly Burke*

How To Use This Guide

Types of Hikes

Loop: A loop hike begins and ends at the same trailhead without duplication of all or most of the route. Round-trip mileage is provided.

Out-and-back: Out-and-back hikes reach a specific destination and return via the same route. Round-trip mileage is provided.

Use trail: A use trail is an obvious footpath that is not maintained by the park or another agency.

How and When to Get There

Joshua Tree National Park is bounded on the south by Interstate 10. The Cottonwood entrance to the park's south end is 65 miles west of Blythe and 52 miles east of Palm Springs. California 62 (Twentynine Palms Highway) winds along the park's northern boundary. The two entrances on the north end are the west entrance south of the town of Joshua Tree and the north entrance just south of Twentynine Palms where the visitor center is located.

Maps and Other Information

The map referred to in the map section for each hike is the Joshua Tree National Park topographic backcountry and hiking map (1:80,000 scale), published by Trails Illustrated/ National Geographic.

In general, the more detailed 7.5-minute USGS quad maps (1:24,000 scale) listed for each hike are not needed unless venturing beyond the described route. Refer to the small-scale maps in this book, especially for shorter nature trails that are typically well signed.

The park entrance fee of $10 per vehicle is valid for seven days. Golden Eagle and Golden Access passes are honored as well.

For current information on park regulations, weather, campgrounds, park resources, and trail conditions contact:

Superintendent
Joshua Tree National Park
74485 National Park Drive
Twentynine Palms, CA 92277
(760) 367-5500

Wildflowers
Wildflowers may begin blooming in the lower elevations of Pinto Basin and along the southern park boundary in February and at higher elevations in March and April. Desert plants above 5,000 feet may bloom as late as June. The Wildflower Hot Line is (760) 767-4684.

Campgrounds
Six of the nine campgrounds in the park are no fee, first-come first-serve. To reserve a campsite in one of the three more developed fee campgrounds in the park call 1-800-365-CAMP (2267).

Website

The park's official website is www.nps.gov/jotr/. You can check the website for weekly ranger programs, including the guided walks that are offered primarily in the spring and fall. The walks are free, with the exception of the 0.5-mile Desert Queen Ranch Tour.

Regulations Pertinent to Day Hiking

Federal law protects all plants and wildlife in the park. No hunting or collecting of any kind is permitted. Gathering firewood or any vegetation is forbidden in the park. Fires are allowed only in established fire rings in the campgrounds.

If you begin your day hike from a backcountry board, it is a good idea to register at the board before setting out.

Dogs and other pets must remain within 100 yards of roads and campgrounds and must be leashed at all times. Because they are not allowed on trails, they are better off left at home.

Respect private land inholdings by closing gates and staying off private land when posted.

Before you begin hiking, be sure to stop at the visitor center or a ranger station to get updated regulations. These rules to enjoy the park by are designed to protect your safety as well as the ecological integrity of Joshua Tree.

Play It Safe

Wandering in the desert has a reputation of being a dangerous activity, thanks to both the Bible and Hollywood. Usually depicted as a wasteland, the desert evokes fear. With proper planning, however, desert hiking is not hazardous. In fact, it is fun, exciting, and quite safe.

An enjoyable desert outing requires preparation. Begin with this book, along with the maps suggested in the hike descriptions, to equip yourself with adequate knowledge about your hiking area.

Calculating the time required for a hike in the desert defies any formula. Terrain is often rough; extensive detours around boulders, dryfalls, and drop-offs mean longer trips. Straight-line distance is an illusion. Sun, heat, and wind likewise all conspire to slow down even the speediest hiker. Therefore, distances are not what they appear in the desert. Five desert miles may take longer than 10 woodland miles. Plan your excursion conservatively.

Regardless of how short a hike may be, it is always wise to carry water. The simple act of breathing can make you very thirsty in the desert air. Of course, carrying water is not enough—take the time to stop and drink it. This is another reason why desert hikes take longer. Frequent water breaks are mandatory. It is best to return from your hike with empty water bottles. You can cut down on loss of bodily moisture by hiking with your mouth closed and breathing through your nose; reduce thirst also by avoiding sweets and alcohol.

Driving to and from the trailhead is statistically far more

dangerous than hiking in the desert backcountry. But being far from the nearest 911 service requires knowledge about possible hazards and proper precautions to avoid them.

Dehydration
Plenty of water is necessary for desert hiking. Carry 1 gallon per person per day in unbreakable plastic screw-top containers, and pause often to drink. Carry water in your car as well so you will have water when you return. As a general rule, plain water is a better thirst-quencher than any of the colored fluids on the market, which usually generate greater thirst. It is very important to maintain proper electrolyte balance by eating small quantities of nutritional foods throughout the day, even if you feel you do not have an appetite.

Weather
Daytime temperatures from June through September average around 100 degrees F. Comfortable hiking weather is the norm during the rest of the year, although May can get toasty. High and low temperatures of 85 and 50 degrees, respectively, typify spring and fall. July and August often bring brief thunderstorms. Winter may bring highs of up to 60 degrees F, along with freezing nights and occasional rain showers. Desert hikers need to be prepared for ever-changing climatic conditions.

The desert is well known for sudden shifts in the weather. The temperature can change 50 degrees F in less than one hour. Prepare yourself with extra food and clothing, rain and wind gear, and a flashlight.

Hypothermia/Hyperthermia

Abrupt chilling is as much a danger in the desert as heat stroke. Storms and/or nightfall can cause desert temperatures to plunge. Wear layers of clothes, adding or subtracting depending on conditions, to avoid overheating or chilling. At the other extreme, you need to protect yourself from sun and wind with proper clothing. The broad-brimmed hat is mandatory equipment for the desert traveler. Even in the cool days of winter, a delightful time in the desert, the sun's rays are intense. Do not forget the sunscreen.

Vegetation

You quickly will learn not to come in contact with certain desert vegetation. Catclaw, Spanish bayonet, and cacti are just a few of the botanical hazards that will get your attention if you become complacent. Carry tweezers to extract cactus spines. Wear long pants if traveling off trail or in a brushy area. Many folks carry a hair comb to assist removal of cholla balls.

Rattlesnakes, Scorpions, and Tarantulas

Unexpected human visitors easily terrify these desert "creepy crawlies," and they react predictably to being frightened. Do not sit or put your hands in dark places you cannot see, especially during the warmer "snake-season" months. Carry and know how to use your snakebite kit for emergencies when help is far away. If bitten, seek medical assistance as quickly as possible. Keep tents zipped and always shake out boots, packs, and clothes before putting them on.

Mine Hazards

Joshua Tree National Park contains hundreds of deserted mines—consider all of them hazardous. When it comes to mines and mine structures, stay out and stay alive. The vast majority of these mines have not been secured or even posted. Keep an eye on young or adventuresome members of your group.

Hantavirus

In addition to the mines, there are often deserted buildings around the mine sites. Hantavirus is a deadly disease carried by deer mice in the Southwest. Any enclosed area increases the chances of breathing the airborne particles that carry this life-threatening virus. As a precaution, do not enter deserted buildings.

Flash Floods

Desert washes and canyons can become traps for unwary visitors when rainstorms hit the desert. Keep a watchful eye on the sky. Never camp in flash flood areas. Check on regional weather conditions at a ranger station before embarking on your backcountry expedition. A storm anywhere upstream in a drainage can cause a sudden torrent in a lower canyon. Do not cross a flooded wash. Both the depth and the current can be deceiving; wait for the flood to recede, which usually does not take long.

Lightning

Be aware of lightning, especially during summer storms. Stay off ridges and peaks. You should also avoid shallow overhangs and gullies, because electrical current often moves at ground level near a lightning strike.

Unstable Rocky Slopes

Desert canyons and mountainsides often consist of crumbly or fragmented rock. Mountain sheep are better adapted to this terrain than we bipeds. Use caution when climbing; however, the downward journey is usually more hazardous. Smooth rock faces such as in slickrock canyons are equally dangerous, especially when you have sand on the soles of your boots. On those rare occasions when they are wet, the rocks are slicker than ice.

Giardia

Any surface water, with the possible exception of springs where they flow out of the ground, is apt to contain *Giardia lamblia*, a microorganism that causes severe diarrhea. Boil water for at least 5 minutes or use a filter system. Iodine drops are not effective in killing this pesky parasite.

Zero Impact

The desert environment is fragile; damage lasts for decades—even centuries. Desert courtesy requires us to leave no evidence that we were ever there. This ethic means no graffiti or defoliation at one end of the spectrum, and no unnecessary footprints on delicate vegetation on the other.

The Falcon Zero-Impact Principles

- *Leave with everything you brought with you.*
- *Leave no sign of your visit.*
- *Leave the landscape as you found it.*

Here are seven general guidelines for desert wilderness behavior:

- Avoid making new trails. If hiking cross-country, stay on one set of footprints when traveling in a group. Try to make your route invisible.
- Desert vegetation grows very slowly. Its destruction leads to wind and water erosion and irreparable harm to the desert. Darker crusty soil that crumbles easily indicates cryptobiotic soils, which are a living blend of tightly bonded mosses, lichens, and bacteria. This dark crust prevents wind and water erosion and protects seeds that fall into the soil. Take special care to avoid stepping on this fragile layer.
- Keep noise down. Desert wilderness means quiet and solitude for both animals and human visitors.
- Leave your pets at home. Joshua Tree regulations forbid

dogs on trails, and no one should leave an animal in a vehicle. Share experiences other than the desert with your best friend.

- Pack it in and pack it out. This is truer in the desert than anywhere else. Desert winds spread debris, and desert air preserves it. Always carry a trash bag, both for your trash and for any that you encounter. If you must smoke, pick up your butts and bag them. Bag and carry out toilet paper (it does not deteriorate in the desert) and feminine hygiene products.

- Treat human waste properly. Bury human waste 4 inches deep and at least 200 feet from water and trails. Do not burn toilet paper; many wildfires have been started this way.

- Respect wildlife. Living in the desert is hard enough without being harassed by human intruders. Be respectful and use binoculars for long-distance viewing. Do not molest the rare desert water sources by playing or bathing in them.

- Respect historical artifacts. Federal law and park regulations forbid disturbing or removing historical evidence over 50 years old. Leave the old miners' things right where they left them so that the explorers who follow you can enjoy the thrill of discovery too.

1
LOST PALMS OASIS

Highlights: A hidden oasis with the largest grove of California fan palms in the park.
Type of hike: Out-and-back.
Total distance: 8 miles.
Elevation gain/loss: 590 feet/690 feet.
Best months: October–April.
Maps: Trails Illustrated Joshua Tree National Park Map; USGS Cottonwood Spring quad.
Parking and trailhead facilities: There is a signed parking area at the end of the paved road.

Finding the trailhead: From California 62 in Twentynine Palms on the north side of the park, take Utah Trail south for 4 miles to the park's north entrance. Continue south on Park Route 12 for 4.8 miles to the Pinto Y intersection. Turn left (south) onto Park Route 11, and go 32 miles to the Cottonwood Visitor Center. Turn left (east), and go 1.5 miles to the Cottonwood Spring parking area.

From the south, take the Cottonwood Canyon exit from Interstate 10, 24 miles east of Indio. Go north for 8 miles to the Cottonwood Visitor Center. Turn right (east), and go 1.5 miles to the Cottonwood Spring parking area.

Key points:
0.0 The trail begins above the oasis at Cottonwood Spring.

Lost Palms Oasis

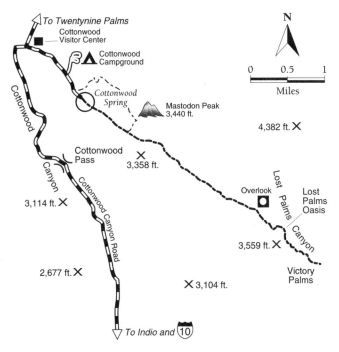

0.9 Mastodon Peak Trail junction is on the left. Continue straight to the oasis.

2.1 The trail descends to the wash.

3.0 Descend down a narrow crumbly ridge to a narrow wash.

4.2 Reach the Palm Oasis overlook.

4.4 Arrive at the floor of the oasis.

5.4 Reach Victory Palms.

The hike: This is a dry, high hike, with no protection from sun and wind. It is a heavily signed route with mileage posts, along with arrows at every bend and every wash crossing.

The trail follows the up-and-down topography of the ridge-and-wash terrain. At each ridge, one hopes to spot the oasis ahead, particularly if it is a hot and sunny day. Not until the final overlook will such hopes be realized. After crossing numerous ridges, descending rocky paths to narrow canyons, and winding up to more ridges, it is a welcome sight!

This is the largest group of California fan palms in Joshua Tree National Park, and they are majestic. This marvelous grove extends about 0.5 mile down the valley. The oasis is within a day-use area to protect bighorn sheep's access to water. You may be lucky enough to spot one of the elusive animals on the rocky slopes above or near the oasis, particularly during hot periods when they are most in need of water. A rocky path leads 0.2 mile from the overlook at 4.2 miles to the oasis. Large boulders, pools of water, intermittent streams, willow thickets, and sandy beaches make this a delightful spot to pause.

Option: The more energetic hiker may wish to continue down the canyon through the willows and around the pools, along an intermittent rusty pipe that was used to channel water to a mining site far to the south. The trail becomes more challenging, with larger boulders to contend with along the way. The Victory Palms are located about 1 mile below the upper end of the Lost Palms Oasis. When your desire for rock scrambling is satisfied, it is time to return to the oasis, and retrace your steps to Cottonwood Spring.

Cottonwood Spring/Morten's Mill Site
Mastodon Peak
Cottonwood Spring Nature Trail

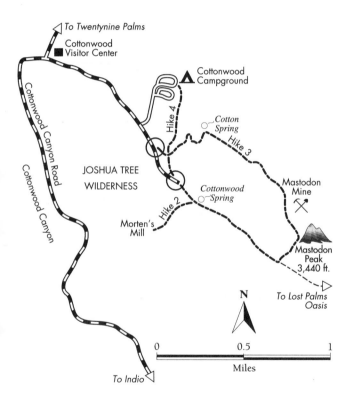

To Twentynine Palms

Cottonwood Visitor Center

Cottonwood Canyon Road

Cottonwood Canyon

Cottonwood Campground

Hike 4

Cotton Spring

Hike 3

JOSHUA TREE WILDERNESS

Cottonwood Spring

Mastodon Mine

Morten's Mill

Hike 2

Mastodon Peak 3,440 ft.

N

To Lost Palms Oasis

To Indio

0   0.5   1

Miles

2
COTTONWOOD SPRING/ MORTEN'S MILL SITE

Highlights: A desert spring, an old mining road, and a historic mine site.
Type of hike: Out-and-back.
Total distance: 1 mile.
Elevation loss: 200 feet.
Best months: October–April.
Maps: Trails Illustrated Joshua Tree National Park Map; USGS Cottonwood Spring quad.
Parking and trailhead facilities: There is a large signed parking area at the end of the paved road.

Finding the trailhead: From Twentynine Palms in the north, take Utah Trail south from California 62 for 4 miles to the park's north entrance. Continue south for 4.8 miles on Park Route 12 and turn left (south) onto Park Route 11 at the Pinto Y intersection (signed for Cottonwood Spring). Drive south for 32 miles to the Cottonwood Campground and visitor center. Turn left (east), and drive 1.5 miles to the parking area. The oasis is down the ramp to the southeast; you can see the palm trees from the parking lot.

From the south, take Interstate 10 east of Indio for 24 miles to the Cottonwood Canyon exit. Turn north and continue for 8 miles to the Cottonwood Campground and visitor center. Turn right (east), and go 1.5 miles to the parking area.

Key points:
0.0 From the parking lot, take the ramp down to the oasis.
0.1 Continue south in the wash.
0.2 Reach Little Chilcoot Pass.
0.5 Arrive at the Morten's Mill site, with a trail post in the center of the wash. This is the turnaround point.

The hike: Cottonwood Spring is a lovely patch of greenery in an otherwise arid landscape. Miners planted the cottonwoods and the fan palms around the turn of the century to make the spring conform to their concept of an oasis. In spite of this unnatural beginning, the sight is satisfying, and obviously the birds enjoy the location.

The hike down the wash provides a display of a wash plant community in the Colorado Desert. Mesquite and smoke trees are dominant. Posts mark the wash segment of the hike.

At 0.25 mile, boulders block the wash. To the right, miners constructed a section of road in the 1880s and their determination to use this route for their vehicles is noteworthy. The ramp is massive, yet even with it in place, the trek up or down the wash must have been arduous with a loaded wagon.

Seeing the mill site at 0.5 mile will cure any thoughts of romanticizing the prospector's life in these parts. While the wash is lovely for its solitude and silence, living here must have been grim. "Cactus" Slim Morten (or Moorten) operated a stamp mill here for less than 10 years. Only rusty equipment and rusting car parts remain.

The hike back up the wash brings you back to the oasis, which looks greener after a sojourn in drier country.

3
MASTODON PEAK

see map page 16

Highlights: A desert spring, a historic mine and mill site, and a monzogranite mound.
Type of hike: Loop.
Total distance: 3 miles.
Elevation gain: 440 feet.
Best months: October–May.
Maps: Trails Illustrated Joshua Tree National Park Map; USGS Cottonwood Spring quad.
Parking and trailhead facilities: The signed parking area is near the campground.

Finding the trailhead: From California 62 in Twentynine Palms in the north, take Utah Trail south for 4 miles to the park's north entrance. Continue 4.8 miles on Park Route 12 to the Pinto Y intersection. Turn left (south) onto Park Route 11 and go south for 32 miles to the Cottonwood Visitor Center. Turn left (east) and go 1.5 miles to the oasis.

From the south, take the Cottonwood Canyon exit, which is 24 miles east of Indio from Interstate 10. Go north for 8 miles to the Cottonwood Visitor Center, then right (east) 1.5 miles to the Cottonwood Spring parking lot.

Walk west from the parking lot, back up the road, for 0.1 mile to the beginning of the nature trail, which is on your right. Walk up the nature trail 0.3 mile to the junction with the Mastodon Peak Trail. From the Cottonwood

1 9

Campground, the trail begins 0.2 mile from campsite 13A on loop A, via the nature trail segment that begins at the campground and meets at the same junction.

Key points:

0.0 Take the nature trail from the parking lot.
0.2 Reach the Mastodon Peak Trail junction and turn right. Pass the Winona Mill ruins and Cotton Spring.
1.0 Arrive at Mastodon Mine. The trail continues above the mine.
1.1 At the trail junction, go left to the peak (0.1-mile round trip).
1.6 Reach the Lost Palms Oasis Trail junction. Turn right to return to the parking area.
2.6 Arrive at Cottonwood Spring. Continue up ramp to parking area.

The hike: A moderate 3-mile loop hike leads from the Cottonwood Spring Oasis to nearby Mastodon Mine, Winona Mill, and Mastodon Peak. The peak requires some scrambling, but it provides impressive views of this southern section of the park, the Eagle Mountains, and Salton Sea.

This trail takes you by two historical sites and to a lofty overlook of the park's southern region. Either approach to the trail includes the nature trail. The view of the old gold mill and the mine is in direct contrast with the Native Americans' use of the riches of the desert; the latter left no ruins or scars on the environment.

Signposts and a rock-lined path clearly mark the trail. The lower section of the hike (0.0 to 0.2 mile) is up a sandy wash to the Winona Mill site. Building foundations and other remnants are all that remain of the mill that refined the gold from the Mastodon Mine in the 1920s. The Hulsey family, who owned the mill and mine, planted the exotic plant specimens at the adjacent Cotton Spring.

The trail winds up the hill above the mill to the Mastodon Mine, which was operated by George Hulsey between 1919 and 1932, when it was abandoned. Carefully thread your way up by the sign above the mine, which is at 1.0 mile. The trail gives you no choice but to pick a path through the mine ruins to the trail post and arrow pointing east on the other side of the mine site. A major freeway-style sign indicates your options and the various distances to the spring, the oasis, and the peak from this point.

The 0.1-mile climb to the peak is on an unsigned trail, although the well-used path is easy to discern, and cairns mark critical spots. This portion of the hike is for the more adventuresome travelers; those for whom it is sufficient to survey Mastodon Peak from below may continue on the trail looping around to the right. The use trail to the peak goes to the right of a boulder pile, across a slab of granite, and winds around to the northeast side of the peak to the summit, on the opposite side from the mine site. Minor boulder scrambling is necessary, but the view is well worth the effort.

After leaving the peak, the trail resumes its zigzag, rocky path through the canyon, well signed with arrows. It is on this portion of the trail that you can clearly see the elephant likeness in the peak behind you. About 0.5 mile beyond the peak, at 1.6 miles, is the intersection with the Lost Palms Oasis Trail. Turn right (northwest) for the 1.1-mile walk down the winding trail to Cotton-wood Spring and the parking lot.

Option: Turn left (southeast) at the intersection of the trail with the Lost Palms Oasis Trail for the longer hike to Lost Palms Oasis (6.3 miles round-trip from this junction and back to the parking lot). Refer to Hike 1 for more information.

4
COTTONWOOD SPRING NATURE TRAIL

see map page 16

Highlights: Identification of desert plants and their use by Native Americans.
Type of hike: Out-and-back.
Total distance: 1 mile.
Elevation gain: Minimal.
Best months: October–April.
Maps: Trails Illustrated Joshua Tree National Park Map; USGS Cottonwood Spring quad.
Parking and trailhead facilities: The parking area is adjacent to the campground.

Finding the trailhead: From California 62 in Twentynine Palms on the north side of the park, take Utah Trail south for 4 miles to the park's north entrance. Continue for 4.8 miles on Park Route 12 to the Pinto Y intersection. Turn left (south) onto Park Route 11 and go south for 32 miles to the Cottonwood Visitor Center. Turn left (east) and go 1.5 miles to the oasis.

From the south, take the Cottonwood Canyon exit, which is 24 miles east of Indio from Interstate 10. Go north for 8 miles to the Cottonwood Visitor Center, then right (east) for 1.5 miles to the Cottonwood Spring parking lot.

From the parking area, walk 0.1 mile west along the road to the nature trail, which is on your right. The nature trail also begins at the eastern ends of loops A and B in the campground and goes to Cottonwood Spring. If you are not camping, however, it is not possible to park at the campground.

Key points:
0.0 Cottonwood Spring Nature Trail trailhead.
0.5 At the Mastodon Peak Trail junction, the trail continues to the campground.

The hike: This broad clear trail leads up a wash from the road near the spring, eventually winding up to a low ridge leading to the campground. This is one of the most informative nature trails in the park. The signs are legible, accurately placed, and highly educational.

The information on this nature trail identifies plants native to the Colorado (Sonoran) Desert. The signs focus on the Cahuilla Indians' use of the plants for food, medicine, and household goods. A Cahuilla elder provided the information. The detailed explanations of the processes used by the original inhabitants create genuine admiration for their sophistication. Several of the plants originally developed by the Native Americans, such as creosote tea and jojoba, are now grown and marketed commercially.

Option: Continue on to the Mastodon Peak Trail (see Hike 3) intersection, which is 0.5 mile up the nature trail from its northern end. You can also walk back down to the parking lot, reviewing the new information you have learned, and visit the Cottonwood Spring, which is located down the ramp at the foot of the parking area.

5
CHOLLA CACTUS GARDEN NATURE TRAIL

Highlights: An unusually dense stand of cholla cactus.
Type of hike: Loop.
Total distance: 0.25 mile.
Elevation gain: Minimal.
Best months: October–April.
Maps: Trails Illustrated Joshua Tree National Park Map; USGS Fried Liver Wash quad.
Parking and trailhead facilities: There is a signed parking area next to the paved highway.

Finding the trailhead: From California 62 in Twentynine Palms, take Utah Trail south for 4 miles to the park's north entrance. Continue for 4.8 miles south on Park Route 12 to the Pinto Y intersection. Turn left (south) onto Park Route 11. The Cholla Cactus Garden parking area is on the right (south) near mile 10, 6.3 miles south of the intersection.

Key points:
0.0 Trailhead.
0.2 Approach the end of the loop.

The hike: This massive array of cholla cacti, common in the Colorado (Sonoran) Desert, is impressive even when it is not in bloom. From mid- to late-February to mid-March,

Cholla Cactus Garden Nature Trail

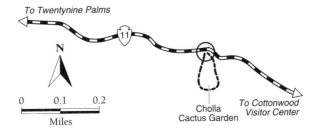

there is intense bee activity at the garden. Those with sensitivity to, or phobias of, bees should avoid visiting here during the pollination season.

This is a self-guided trail but often there may be no brochures available, so the numbers posted on the trail only tantalize the visitor. Even without a pamphlet for interpretation, the high density of Bigelow cholla, known as "teddy bear cactus," is impressive. The sea of cholla extends well beyond the garden's fenced area. Panoramic views of the surrounding Hexie Mountains, the Pinto Range, and the vast Pinto Basin combine to make the Cholla Cactus Garden a spectacular spot on the edge of this southern desert region.

6
SAND DUNES

Highlights: Remote sand dunes in a broad desert basin.
Type of hike: Out-and-back.
Total distance: 2.5 miles.
Elevation gain: Minimal.
Best months: January–April.
Maps: Trails Illustrated Joshua Tree National Park Map; USGS Pinto Mountain quad.
Parking and trailhead facilities: The backcountry board (kiosk) and parking area are alongside the paved highway.

Finding the trailhead: The route takes off from the Turkey Flat backcountry board, which is on the east side of Park Route 11. The trailhead is 16.2 miles south of the Pinto Y intersection, and 27.5 miles north of the Cottonwood Visitor Center.

Key points:
0.0 Turkey Flat backcountry board.
1.2 Reach the sand dunes.

The hike: From the Turkey Flat backcountry board, head northeast toward the high point on the distant horizon, the 3,983-foot Pinto Mountain. You can see the sand dunes about a mile away, appearing as a low-lying dark ridge or

Sand Dunes

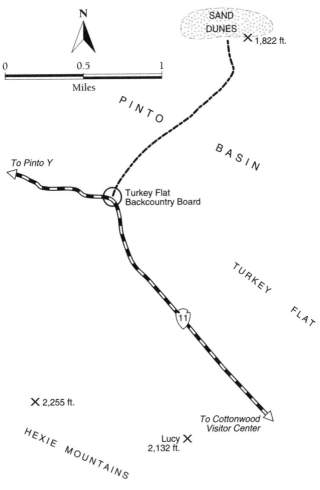

mound in this otherwise flat stretch of Colorado Desert in the Pinto Basin.

Begin by heading 0.2 mile up a large wash that leads to a circular sand bowl. Continue northeasterly for another mile across a creosote-brittlebush flat to the sand dunes. This is a delightful place to visit during winter and in the spring, especially when primrose and other wildflowers are in bloom. Spend some quiet time here, wandering along this wind-swept uplift of sand, reflecting on how the ever-present desert winds have both created and kept in place these dunes over thousands of years. The setting is equally impressive. The dunes are on the edge of the austere lowlands of a vast desert basin ringed by stark mountains, creating a sense of limit-less space.

To return, simply walk toward the highest point to the southwest, which is the crest of the Hexie Mountains, and you will soon end up back at the backcountry board.

Pushwalla Pass

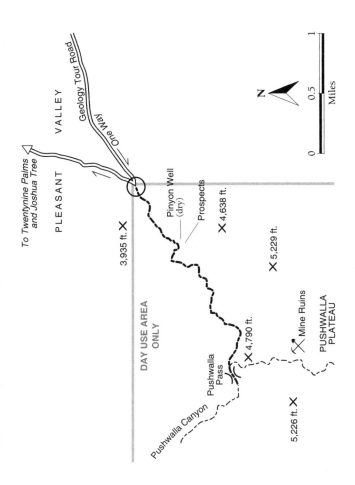

7
PUSHWALLA PASS

Highlights: Historic stone wall mining structures, Joshua trees on a high plateau in a secluded corner of the park, and wide vistas.
Type of hike: Out-and-back.
Total distance: 5.6 miles.
Elevation gain: 1,060 feet.
Best months: October–May.
Maps: Trails Illustrated Joshua Tree National Park Map; USGS Malapai Hill quad.
Parking and trailhead facilities: The parking area and unsigned trail are adjacent to the rough dirt road.

Finding the trailhead: From Twentynine Palms in the north, take Utah Trail south from California 62 for 4 miles to the park's north entrance. Continue south for 4.8 miles on Park Route 12 to the Pinto Y intersection. Stay to the right (southwest) on Park Route 12 and drive another 5.1 miles to Geology Tour Road, which is signed "Squaw Tank" at the turnoff. From the west entrance, the turnoff is 15.1 miles southeast of Joshua Tree. Turn south on Geology Tour Road, which is rough but usually passable for standard vehicles. The unsigned trailhead is 10.2 miles south on Geology Tour Road next to the 15 km post. Park at the Pinyon Well parking area and begin the hike up the wash.

Key points:
0.0 Pinyon Well Trailhead.
0.8 Reach the Pinyon Well site.
1.2 The canyon forks; stay left up the main wash.
2.8 Arrive at Pushwalla Pass.

The hike: This is a varied hike with several side options into a remote and lightly used region of the park. The entire trip takes place in an area limited to day use for wildlife protection.

The trail starts up a wash near the mouth of the "Pinyon Well" Canyon, which drains east from Pushwalla Pass. The country is characterized by scattered juniper and Joshua trees, punctuated with spires of columnar rocks overlooking the canyon. The wash forks at 0.3 mile; stay right.

At 0.8 mile the canyon narrows just below the remains of a water trough and concrete foundations at Pinyon Well. A mine shaft is fenced off for public safety. Early prospectors built a stamp mill at Pinyon Well to separate gold from ore that was hauled in from nearby mines. Birds and other wildlife are attracted by water seeps at the old well. At 1 mile a rockslide blocks the canyon; cut left on a use trail which quickly leads back to the wash. Look here for the remnants of the original asphalt roadway built by the miners.

At 1.2 miles the canyon again forks; stay left up the main wash. At 1.6 miles a pinyon-juniper wash dotted with Joshua trees enters from the left (south). For an expansive view of the canyon, take a short 0.2-mile walk up the open wash to where heavy brush makes further hiking difficult.

At 1.9 miles the wash forks, with the trail to Pushwalla Pass continuing to the left. At 2.2 miles, avoid another rockslide blocking the wash by taking the use trail to the left. At 2.4 miles the wash again forks; the smaller wash to the right (west) is the route to Pushwalla Pass.

Continue up the wash another 0.4 mile to 4,660-foot Pushwalla Pass. An iron post gate marks the pass. Hold onto your hat, for the pass is truly a classic high desert wind funnel, decorated with pinyon-juniper and live oak. If the pass is your goal, backtrack to complete this 5.6-mile round trip.

Options: For a 0.8-mile round trip to some historic mining ruins (shown on the topographic map) head up the left-hand wash at mile 2.4. After one-tenth of a mile, climb toward the right-hand canyon on the right side of the draw. Soon you will see the largely overgrown mining trail up ahead. Follow it another 0.2 mile to the two roofless rock houses that sit just above a wet spring.

Pushwalla Plateau is well worth exploring from Pushwalla Pass. Take an old mining trail to the south uphill about 50 yards east of the pass; several cairns mark the spot. The trail is steep in places but easy to follow. At 0.8 mile the trail passes mining remains, including a rock building foundation. This is potentially a hazardous area because of unsecured vertical mineshafts nearby. The trail begins to fade out here; simply continue straight, angling upward to the left (east) for another 0.2 mile to the 5,200-foot crest of the Pushwalla Plateau ridge, where Joshua trees and rock mounds characterize the landscape. Savor the spectacular views southward to the Salton Sea and in every direction in these remote Little San Bernardino Mountains. Seldom visited ridges and canyons radiate below and there is always the wind to keep you company.

8
KEYS VIEW AND INSPIRATION PEAK

Highlights: Spectacular views, an interpretive sign with information on air pollution in Joshua Tree.
Type of hike: Loop with an out-and-back leg.
Total distance: 0.25-mile loop plus 1.5-mile out-and-back for peak hike.
Elevation gain: Minimal for loop, 525 feet for the peak.
Best months: October–June.
Maps: Trails Illustrated Joshua Tree National Park Map; USGS Keys View quad.
Parking and trailhead facilities: You will find a paved parking area, informational signs, and restrooms at the trailhead.

Finding the trailhead: From California 62 in the town of Joshua Tree, take Park Boulevard south for 1 mile to where it becomes Quail Springs Road; continue for 4.3 miles to the park's west entrance. Follow Park Route 12 for 11.2 miles to the Keys View Road (Park Route 13), which continues to the right (south). Turn south on Keys View Road; go 5.8 miles to end of the road.

Key points:
0.0 The trailhead is at the north end of the Keys View parking area.
0.5 Ascend to the first summit (5,558 feet).

Keys View and Inspiration Peak

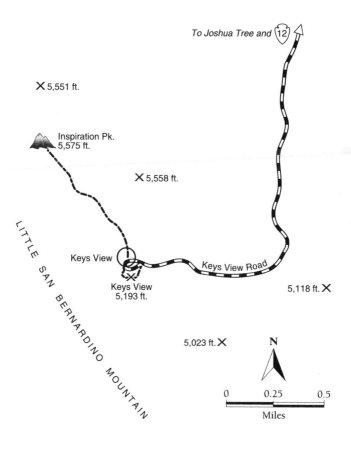

To Joshua Tree and (12)

✕ 5,551 ft.

Inspiration Pk.
5,575 ft.

✕ 5,558 ft.

Keys View

Keys View Road

Keys View
5,193 ft.

5,118 ft. ✕

LITTLE SAN BERNARDINO MOUNTAIN

5,023 ft. ✕

N

| 0 | 0.25 | 0.5 |

Miles

0.6 Reach the saddle (5,460 feet).

0.7 Approach the summit of Inspiration Peak (5,575 feet).

The hike: The clear, paved, barrier-free Keys View path is the highest trail in the park accessible by a paved road. You can count on a brisk breeze, so bring your windbreaker.

The viewpoint is on the crest of the Little San Bernardino Mountains and provides an expansive view of the Coachella Valley and the San Bernardino Range to the west. Unfortunately, pollution from the Los Angeles Basin often obscures the view. Information boards contrasting smog levels give the viewer a good idea of how air pollution affects visibility at differing distances. The smog also endangers the biological integrity of the park itself.

At the lookout there is no diagrammatic map of the park or explanation of the area's geology, a situation often creating questions from visitors to Keys View. Either schedule this trip for late in your stay at Joshua Tree so you will be familiar with the park's landmarks, or bring your park map with you.

A short side trip to Inspiration Peak makes an enjoyable addition for those who like to hike even higher. A hiker symbol marks the trailhead on the north (right) side of the parking area at Keys View. The somewhat steep, rocky trail is well worn and in good condition. Nearly 400 feet are gained to a false summit in the first 0.5-mile.

Look carefully for the trail continuing to the right. It drops 100 feet into a saddle at 0.6 mile, and then climbs around the left side, gaining 120 feet in the next 0.25 mile. Keys View sits far below to the south, as do the Coachella

Valley and prominent peaks of the higher San Bernardino Range. The added perspective gained on the steep canyons and high ridges makes this steep, short climb more than worthwhile. An easily followed use trail continues another 0.1 mile northwest along the main crest until it reaches a mound of large boulders. From Inspiration Peak at 0.75 mile, double back on the trail leading down to the Keys View parking area.

Option: You can extend the Inspiration Peak hike by scrambling over the rocks and dropping into another saddle containing a small storage shed. Climb cross-country up the ridgeline to the next high point, which offers even broader views of the park stretching west and north to the Wonderland of Rocks.

9
LOST HORSE MINE

Highlights: A large historic mine, superb views of the Wonderland of Rocks, Malapai Hill, and the vast expanse of Pleasant Valley.
Type of hike: Out-and-back.
Total distance: 4 miles.
Elevation gain: 400 feet.
Best months: October–May.
Maps: Trails Illustrated Joshua Tree National Park Map; USGS Keys View quad.
Parking and trailhead facilities: The parking area is adjacent to a dirt road.

Finding the trailhead: From California 62 in the town of Joshua Tree, take Park Boulevard south for 1 mile to where it becomes Quail Springs Road; continue for 4.3 miles to the park's west entrance. Follow Park Route 12 for 11.2 miles to the Keys View Road (Park Route 13), which continues to the right (south). Keys View Road is 20 miles southwest of the Oasis Visitor Center at Twentynine Palms by way of Park Route 12. Continue south on the Keys View Road for 2.6 miles to the signed Lost Horse Mine Road. Turn left (southeast) and drive to the Lost Horse Mine Trailhead, which is at the end of this 1.1-mile-long dirt road.

Lost Horse Mine

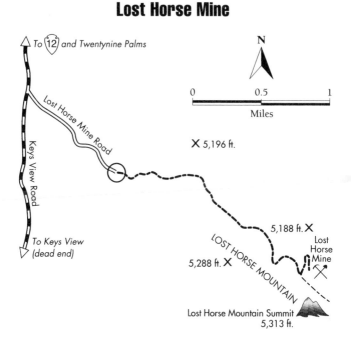

Key points:
0.0 Lost Horse Mine Trailhead.
2.0 Reach Lost Horse Mine.

The hike: This multifaceted hike offers a pleasant out-and-back journey to a large mining complex with optional side trips to several high panoramic points.

The clear, wide, but somewhat rocky trail climbs moderately, gaining 300 feet after 1 mile across high desert swales of juniper, yucca, a few stunted Joshua trees, and nolina (commonly called bear grass), a member of the agave family often mistaken for yucca because of its long spearlike leaves.

At 2 miles the two-track trail reaches the lower end of Lost Horse Mine. This is the largest essentially intact historic mining site in the park and you could easily spend several hours here studying rock buildings, mineshafts, a large wooden 10-stamp mill, and a winch above the mill used to lower miners and equipment into the mine. The largest mineshaft, some 500 feet deep, is covered. However, other smaller ones remain unsecured on the hillsides so you should be extremely cautious when wandering around this site.

This was one of the most profitable mines in the park. A German miner named Frank Diebold made the first strike. He was later bought out by prospector Johnny Lang who happened onto the strike in 1893 while searching for a lost horse. He and his partners began developing the mine two years later. Their process involved crushing the ore at the mill and then mixing it with "quicksilver" mercury, which bonded with the gold so that it could be separated from the ore rock. Lang was later forced to sell his share of the mine to Jep Ryan. The end came in 1924 when the now-elderly Lang died of starvation while walking out from his remote cabin.

After visiting the mine, double back the way you came for an enjoyable round trip.

Options: For a bird's-eye view of the mine and its surroundings, hike north 0.2 mile on the two-track which climbs above the fenced-off stamp mill. A short use trail continues up to Lost Horse Point (5,188 feet), which affords a magnificent panorama of surrounding basins and peaks, including the Wonderland of Rocks to the north. From here you can see a track running southeast to a pass. Using care on the loose rocks, drop down this trail and walk 0.2 mile to the pass if you want to climb 5,313-foot Lost Horse Mountain. From the pass, climb southwest 0.3 mile up the ridge, gaining 200 feet, to the long ridgetop that forms the summit of the mountain. A faint use trail is easier seen coming down than going up, but climbing is easy on or off the use trail.

10
ARCH ROCK NATURE TRAIL

Highlights: White Tank granite formations and geology lessons.
Type of hike: Loop.
Total distance: 0.3 mile.
Elevation gain: Minimal.
Best months: October–April.
Maps: Trails Illustrated Joshua Tree National Park Map; USGS Malapai Hill quad.
Parking and trailhead facilities: The signed trailhead is adjacent to the campground.

Finding the trailhead: From California 62 in Twentynine Palms, take Utah Trail south for 4 miles to the park's north entrance. Continue south on Park Route 12 for 4.8 miles to the Pinto Y intersection. Turn left (south) at the Y intersection onto Park Route 11, and go 2.8 miles to White Tank Campground, which is on your left (east). Turn into the campground, and follow the inconspicuous nature trail sign to the trailhead, on the left immediately after the campground information board.

Key points:
0.0 Arch Rock Nature Trail trailhead.
0.1 Reach Arch Rock.
0.3 Return to the trailhead.

Arch Rock Nature Trail

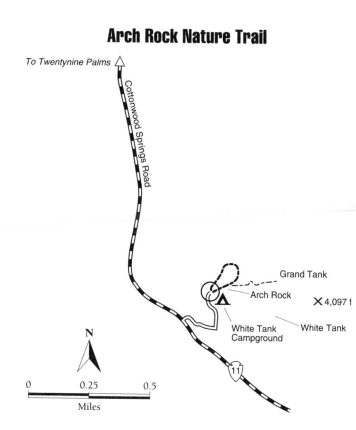

To Twentynine Palms

Cottonwood Springs Road

Grand Tank

Arch Rock

✕ 4,097 f

White Tank Campground

White Tank

N

11

| 0 | 0.25 | 0.5 |

Miles

The hike: This nature trail focuses on the unique geology of the fascinating rock formations that abound in this area of the park. The informational signs present a sophisticated series of geology lessons, far beyond the simplistic rock identification usually found on such trails. The trail itself is an adventure in geology as it winds through fantastic boulders to the famed Arch Rock at 0.1 mile.

A trip through the geology lesson covers igneous rock formation, the origins of White Tank granite, erosion, selective erosion, dikes, faults, and how natural arches are formed. The remainder of your visit in the park will be greatly enhanced by this knowledge.

Options: A side trip from Arch Rock through the slot to the northeast leads to an old, sanded-in cattle tank that has created good habitat for birds and other desert creatures.

You might also want to visit the Twin Tanks, which are 1 mile directly east of White Tank Campground. Like Arch Rock, the granite formations are gracefully sculpted by the forces of weather and are inviting to explore. Twin Tanks also has two partially buried old tank sites.

11
SKULL ROCK NATURE TRAIL

Highlights: A Joshua tree forest and unusual jumbo rock formations, with periodic informational signs.
Type of hike: Loop.
Total distance: 1.7 miles.
Elevation gain: Minimal.
Best months: October–April.
Maps: Trails Illustrated Joshua Tree National Park Map; USGS Malapai Hill quad.
Parking and trailhead facilities: The signed nature trail is adjacent to the paved highway.

Finding the trailhead: From California 62 in Twentynine Palms, take Utah Trail south for 4 miles to the park's north entrance; continue south on Park Route 12 for 4.8 miles to the Pinto Y intersection. Bear right (southwest), still on PR 12, and continue 3.7 miles to the signed Skull Rock Nature Trail trailhead.

Key points:
0.0 Skull Rock Nature Trail trailhead.
0.7 Reach the Jumbo Rocks Campground entrance.
1.2 Come to the end of campground loop E.
1.7 Complete the loop on PR 12.

Skull Rock Nature Trail
Crown Prince Lookout

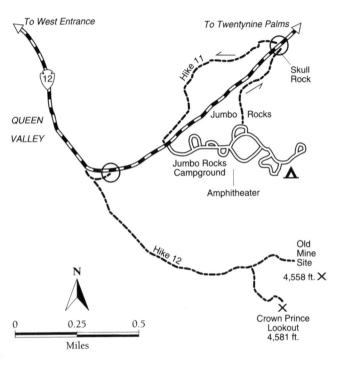

To West Entrance

To Twentynine Palms

Hike 11

Skull Rock

12

QUEEN VALLEY

Jumbo Rocks

Jumbo Rocks Campground

Amphitheater

N

Old Mine Site

4,558 ft. ✕

Hike 12

✕ Crown Prince Lookout 4,581 ft.

0   0.25   0.5

Miles

The hike: Park Road 12 divides this loop trail. The northern half of the loop begins at the Skull Rock sign on the highway and starts out northward; at 0.7 mile it ends at the Jumbo Rocks Campground entrance. To pick up the other half of the trail from there, it is necessary to walk down 0.5 mile through the campground to the end of loop E.

The northern half of the loop has not been renovated recently by the park. The route meanders along parallel to the road, winding between rock formations and through shallow gullies. There are several interpretive signs but most are so weathered they are illegible. The trail is haphazardly marked with rocks but can always be discerned in the sandy soil. While the eroded boulders are spectacular sights, the information provided is not thematic. Basic geology, plant identification, and desert survival tips are intermixed.

Cross the road at the Jumbo Rocks Campground at 0.7 mile, then follow the road through the campground to the southern section of the trail, which begins at a sign on loop E at 1.2 miles. On the southern half of the loop, the interpretive signs are recent, more plentiful, and more instructive. They focus on desert diversity and the interconnectedness of the plants and animals that make this region their home. The famous, aptly named, and much-photographed Skull Rock sits at the end of the southern loop, immediately adjacent to the road. Skull Rock itself is quite forbidding, and the other formations on the route are equally fascinating and thought-provoking. This is an excellent family outing for photography and for leisurely exploration.

12
CROWN PRINCE LOOKOUT

see map page 46

Highlights: Scenic overlook of Twin Tanks, Arch Rock, Queen Valley, and the Pinto Range.
Type of hike: Out-and-back.
Total distance: 3 miles.
Elevation gain: Minimal.
Best months: October–April.
Maps: Trails Illustrated Joshua Tree National Park Map; USGS Malapai Hill quad.
Parking and trailhead facilities: The visitor parking area is at the Jumbo Rocks Campground near the unsigned trailhead.

Finding the trailhead: From California 62 in Twentynine Palms, take Utah Trail south for 4 miles to the park's north entrance; continue south on Park Route 12 for 4.8 miles to the Pinto Y intersection. Bear right (southwest) and continue on PR 12 for another 3.7 miles to Jumbo Rocks Campground. Park in the visitor lot at the entrance, or park along the north side of the road, and walk east along the road shoulder for 0.25 mile to the trailhead at the sharp curve in the road just west of the campground. The unsigned trailhead is marked by six huge stones that have been positioned to block vehicle access to this former jeep route.

Key points:

0.0 The trailhead is on PR 12.

1.3 At the trail junction, turn right (south) to the vista, left (east) to the old mine site.

1.5 Reach the overlook.

The hike: This pleasant hike follows a well-defined old jeep track up a broad sandy ridge. At 1.3 miles the trail splits at a Y intersection. To the right (south) the track heads for a huge boulder pile; do not be intimidated, the trail curves to an adjacent promontory and does not climb the peak. From the vista point at 1.5 miles, you can see the valleys to the east and the vast White Tank granite formations that lie between here and the Pinto Mountains. This option is 0.2 mile from the Y intersection.

Back at the Y intersection, the left (east) trail is also a gentle 0.2-mile-long track. It ends in a broad sandy turn-around. A footpath continues to the right of a more modest boulder pile and ends at the old mine site.

Though the elevation gain is minimal, the walk back to PR 12 is entirely downhill.

Ryan Mountain
Cap Rock Nature Trail

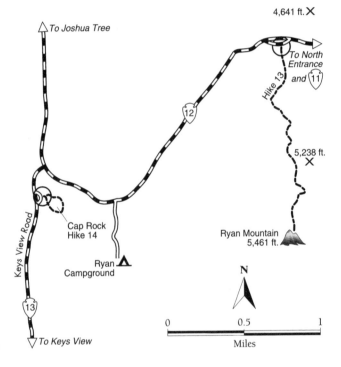

4,641 ft. ✕

△ To Joshua Tree

To North
Entrance
and (11)

Hike 13

12

5,238 ft.
✕

Keys View Road

Cap Rock
Hike 14

Ryan Mountain
5,461 ft.

Ryan
Campground

N

13

▽ To Keys View

0   0.5   1

Miles

13
RYAN MOUNTAIN

Highlights: A panoramic view from the center of the park.
Type of hike: Out-and-back.
Total distance: 3 miles.
Elevation gain: 1,070 feet.
Best months: October–May.
Maps: Trails Illustrated Joshua Tree National Park Map; USGS Indian Cove and Keys View quads.
Parking and trailhead facilities: You will find a paved parking area at the signed trailhead.

Finding the trailhead: From California 62 in Joshua Tree, drive south on Park Boulevard for 1 mile to where it turns into Quail Springs Road. Continue 4 miles to the park's west entrance. Follow Park Route 12 for 12.5 miles to Ryan Mountain Trailhead on your right (south). The signed parking area is 2.1 miles east of the junction with Keys View Road.

Key points:
0.0 Ryan Mountain Trailhead.
0.4 The trail begins a steep climb.
1.5 Reach the summit of Ryan Mountain.

The hike: The trail leaves from the parking area through a massive boulder gate of White Tank granite sculpted by selective erosion. This well-signed official park trail is quite a display of rock workmanship. Steeper portions of the trail, beginning at 0.4 mile, feature stair steps artfully constructed from the plentiful native rocks, so it is easy walking up, and there is no skidding going down. The slopes of Ryan Mountain are dotted with ancient metamorphic rocks of schist and gneiss, perhaps several hundred million years old. The trail winds around the hill from the trailhead, and takes a relatively gentle slope to the peak, which is at 1.5 miles.

If you have spent several days walking nature trails, visiting mine sites, and hiking canyon washes, this 5,461-foot-high peak provides a welcome aerial view of the central portion of the park, including Lost Horse, Queen, and Pleasant Valleys. While enjoying the scenery you can also enjoy reading and signing the peak register. On your return, don't miss the Indian Cave sites at the western end of the parking area. A sign indicates their location. The fire-stained rock shelters provide a reminder of the centuries of use by the human visitors that this silent land has seen.

14
CAP ROCK NATURE TRAIL

see map page 50

Highlights: Interesting monzogranite rock formations.
Type of hike: Loop (wheelchair accessible).
Total distance: 0.4 mile.
Elevation gain: Minimal.
Best months: October–May.
Maps: Trails Illustrated Joshua Tree National Park Map; USGS Keys View quad.
Parking and trailhead facilities: Both the parking area and trail are signed and paved.

Finding the trailhead: From California 62 in Joshua Tree, take the Park Boulevard exit south for 1 mile to where it turns into Quail Springs Road, and continue for 4 miles to the park's west entrance. Continue on Park Route 12 for 15 miles to the right turn on Keys View Road. The Cap Rock parking area is on the east (left) side of the road, 0.1 mile from the intersection.

Key points:
0.0 Trailhead.
0.4 Complete the loop.

The hike: This level nature trail is paved and wheelchair accessible, although it has weathered considerably since it was built in 1982. The numerous signs have also weathered; some are almost illegible. The focus of the information is on the desert plants that grow around these fascinating quartz monzonite boulder piles. Cap Rock is nearby, with its sporty visor-shaped wedge resembling the bill on a baseball cap. Frequent use by rock climbers makes the 0.4-mile long Cap Rock Trail an interesting scene, with the silhouettes of climbers like dots against the sky.

15
LUCKY BOY VISTA

Highlights: A view of the Split Rock region of north-central Joshua Tree.
Type of hike: Out-and-back.
Total distance: 2.5 miles.
Elevation gain: Minimal.
Best months: October–April.
Maps: Trails Illustrated Joshua Tree National Park Map; USGS Queen Mountain quad.
Parking and trailhead facilities: There is a gated dirt road and parking area at the trailhead.

Finding the trailhead: From California 62 in Twentynine Palms, take Utah Trail south for 4 miles to the park's north entrance; continue 4.8 miles on Park Route 12 to the Pinto Y intersection. Bear right and stay on PR 12 another 5.1 miles to a dirt road on your right (directly opposite Geology Tour Road, which goes south). Turn north on the dirt road for 0.8 mile to a gated road going east. Park there.

Key points:
0.0 Head east from the trailhead on the wide sandy two-track.
1.0 Reach the gate; continue around it on the two-track.
1.2 The mine site is on the right. The overlook is 0.5 mile beyond.

Lucky Boy Vista, Desert Queen Mine and Wash, and Pine City Site

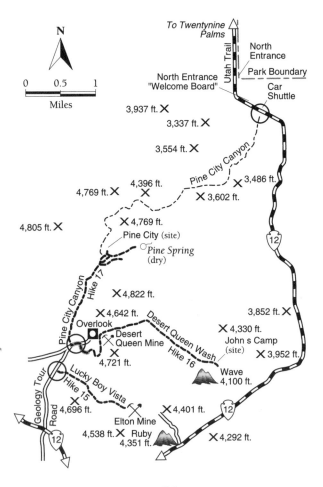

N

0   0.5   1
Miles

To Twentynine Palms

Utah Trail

North Entrance

Park Boundary

Car Shuttle

North Entrance "Welcome Board"

3,937 ft. ✕

3,337 ft. ✕

3,554 ft. ✕

Pine City Canyon

✕ 3,486 ft.

4,769 ft. ✕   4,396 ft. ✕   ✕ 3,602 ft.

4,805 ft. ✕   ✕ 4,769 ft.

Pine City (site)

○ *Pine Spring* (dry)

✕ 4,822 ft.

Pine City Canyon

Hike 17

✕ 4,642 ft.

Overlook

Desert Queen Wash   Hike 16

Desert Queen Mine ✕

✕ 4,721 ft.

3,852 ft. ✕

✕ 4,330 ft.

John s Camp (site)

✕ 3,952 ft.

Wave 4,100 ft.

12

Geology Tour Road

Lucky Boy Vista   Hike 15

✕ 4,696 ft.

Elton Mine

✕ 4,401 ft.

12

4,538 ft. ✕   Ruby 4,351 ft.

✕ 4,292 ft.

12

The hike: This relatively flat hike to the Elton Mine site is on a broad sandy jeep track that is in better shape than the Geology Tour Road extension you take to get here. The trail climbs gradually above a yucca and pinyon boulder garden to the north. At 1 mile continue around the gate. You will see the fenced-off mineshafts on your right at 1.2 miles. Just beyond the mine, on a lofty plateau, is a magnificent overlook of the Split Rock region of the park. For a short hike, this outing provides an opportunity for desert solitude, a great view, and a historical site.

The views on the trip back to the car are equally wide-ranging.

16
DESERT QUEEN MINE AND WASH

see map page 56

Highlights: Largest and longest operating mine in the park, additional mines, and miners' settlements.
Type of hike: Out-and-back.
Total distance: 4 miles.
Elevation loss: Minimal to overlook and mine sites; 580 feet for wash walk.
Best months: October–April.
Maps: Trails Illustrated Joshua Tree National Park Map; USGS Queen Mountain quad.
Parking and trailhead facilities: There is a parking area and back-country board (kiosk) at the end of the dirt road.

Finding the trailhead: From California 62 in Twentynine Palms, take Utah Trail south for 4 miles to the park's north entrance; continue 4.8 miles on Park Route 12 to the Pinto Y intersection. Stay to the right (southwest) on Park Route 12 and drive 5.1 miles to a right turn on a dirt road immediately opposite the signed Geology Tour Road, which heads south ("Squaw Tank" is the sign at the intersection). Turn north on the one-lane dirt road, and drive 1.4 miles to its end at the Pine City backcountry board and parking area.

Key points:

0.0 At the trailhead, a cable barricade deters vehicles. The broad trail goes east.

0.3 Pass the old stone ruins of a miner's dwelling, the rocky trail winds down to the wash.

0.6 Pass mining sites.

1.3 Huge boulders totally block the wash. Take a crude trail on the bank to the right (west).

1.5 The wash widens; an old prospector site is on a low shelf to the right.

1.8 Another boulder tumble blocks the narrow wash. Follow cairns to the left.

2.0 Bear right to John's Camp site on the low bank.

The hike: This interesting trip covers a variety of mine sites, from the most prosperous in the area (Desert Queen) to those that were obviously not successful. The Desert Queen was in operation from 1895 to 1961 and was one of the most productive gold mines in the southern California desert. While mine entrances dot the mountainside at the site, the magnitude of the Desert Queen operation is most evident from the massive tailings that drip like blood down the mountain into the wash below. The debris that is left around the site—and that continues to appear miles down the wash—is also evidence of the environmental repercussions of this industrial use of the desert.

The experience of hiking down the wash erases the sight of the damage to the mountainside. The huge boulders that rise above you—and periodically are in front of you in the wash, blocking your way at 1.3 and 1.8 miles—are reminders of the forces of nature that are still in operation. The wash's vegetation is profuse and diverse. Mesquite, creosote, and smoke trees line the wash, sometimes even blocking your passage. The intermittent power of rushing water scours the wash, but these durable plants enjoy this location.

The mining sites farther down the wash represent the other end of the economic spectrum from the Desert Queen. Unlike this operation, the other sites are small. The artifacts found around the miners' dwellings indicate a grim existence for these workers. This was primitive living. The size of the tailings shows that the excavations were not extensive. These mining projects did not last long.

As you walk back up the wash after visiting John's Camp at 2.0 miles, you can again revel in the beauty of the canyon. Then, turning the last corner, you encounter the mining equipment left in the wash by the Desert Queen. Joshua Tree National Park preserves two different worlds. We can learn much by being aware of both of them.

Options: You can shorten the hike to a 1.2-mile round trip to an overlook, or a 2.2-mile out-and-back hike to mine sites. In both instances, the elevation gain is minimal.

17
PINE CITY SITE

see map page 56

Highlights: A picturesque former mining camp, rock formations, and a scenic canyon.
Type of hike: Out-and-back.
Total distance: 3.4 miles.
Elevation gain: Minimal.
Best months: October–May.
Maps: Trails Illustrated Joshua Tree National Park Map; USGS Queen Mountain quad.
Parking and trailhead facilities: There is parking space and a backcountry board (kiosk) at the end of the dirt road.

Finding the trailhead: From California 62 in Twentynine Palms, take Utah Trail south for 4 miles to the park's north entrance; continue 4.8 miles on Park Route 12 to the Pinto Y intersection. Stay right (southwest) on Park Route 12 for 5.1 miles to the unsigned dirt road on your right (directly opposite Geology Tour Road). Turn right (north) on the dirt road and go 1.4 miles to the road's end at the Pine City backcountry board.

Key points:
0.0 Pine City backcountry board and trailhead.
1.1 At the trail junction continue left; the right-hand trail leads to an old mine site.
1.6 The right-hand trail leads to Pine Spring; continue left.
1.7 Reach the Pine City site.

Optional extended hike:
2.2 The trail ends on a ridge above Pine City Canyon.
2.3 A use trail drops to Pine City Canyon.

The hike: This is a mellow out-and-back hike to the picturesque "day-use-only" former mining camp of Pine City. The optional continuation makes for a more difficult hike past the Pine City site and down into the head of a colorful canyon, with several steep rock pitches.

Except for a few mineshafts grated over for public safety, all that remains of Pine City is the wind rustling through the pines. Still, the short, gentle walk to the Pine City site provides ample opportunities for exploration and for savoring its bouldery beauty. The trail maintains an even grade across a high Mojave Desert plateau covered with Joshua trees.

At mile 1.1, an obscure trail leads to the right for 0.3 mile to a picture-perfect pocket of monzoquartz granite ringed with pinyon pines. The main trail to Pine City continues left (north). At 1.6 miles another trail takes off to the right (east), dropping 100 feet in 0.2 mile to the dry Pine Spring. The spring lies just above the narrow notch of a steep, boulder-strewn canyon. This pleasant spot is well suited for a picnic or for just plain relaxing. Bighorn sheep rely on the cool shelter of this place when people are not there.

From the Pine City turnoff, continue left (north) another 0.1 mile to the Pine City site, which is immediately east of the trail in a wide, sandy flat next to a huge round boulder sitting atop a rock platform. You could easily spend several hours poking around the myriad of side canyons and interesting rock formations that surround the Pine City site. The site contains at least one grated mineshaft and at least one more that is unsecured, so indeed caution should be exercised. Return the way you came to complete this level out-and-back hike.

Option: To extend the hike into the upper reaches of Pine City Canyon, stay left (north) on the trail to a point 0.5 mile northeast of the Pine City site, where the trail ends on a ridge next to a small hill. Drop into the broad saddle southwest of the 4,769-foot hill shown on the topographic map. If time and energy permit, this hill provides an easy walk-up for a stunning view in all directions. From the saddle, drop down the steep gully to the main Pine Canyon wash at 4,350 feet and 2.3 miles. A few cairns mark the way.

The head of Pine City Canyon is spectacular, lined with great columns of gray and red rock. The canyon drops steeply, requiring boulder hopping and, at times, the use of "all fours" to negotiate the steep but stable rocks. For out-and-back hikers wishing to sample a bit of this steep-walled canyon, hike a mile or so down to about the 4,000-foot level to a good turnaround point. This upper stretch harbors the deepest and most dramatic section of the canyon. Below 4,000 feet the canyon narrows and steepens with several more difficult rock sections requiring skill and agility with both hands and feet. Here, the canyon is trending east to northeast and dropping about 500 feet per mile. Multicolored bands of rippled rock—purple, red, yellow—grace the floor of a canyon lined with barrel cacti.

Note: To avoid disturbing the sheep and other wildlife, the Pine City/Pine Spring/upper Pine City Canyon area is within a much larger day-use-only area. Camping is currently allowed south of Pine City in accordance with park regulations. Check at the visitor center in case these boundaries are altered.

18
FORTYNINE PALMS OASIS

Highlights: Towering California fan palms in a remote location.
Type of hike: Out-and-back.
Total distance: 3 miles.
Elevation gain: 360 feet.
Best months: October–April.
Maps: Trails Illustrated Joshua Tree National Park Map; USGS Queen Mountain quad.
Parking and trailhead facilities: This is a signed end-of-road trailhead.

Finding the trailhead: From California 62, 11.2 miles east of Park Boulevard in Joshua Tree, take Fortynine Palms Canyon Road south for 2 miles to its end. From Twentynine Palms, travel 5.5 miles west on CA 62 to the Fortynine Palms Canyon Road exit, then go south for 2 miles to the road's end at the parking area.

Key points:
0.0 Trailhead.
0.3 The trail turns sharply to the right; continue climbing.
0.5 Climb to the top of the ridge; achieve the first view of the oasis.
1.0 Cross the wash; continue downhill.
1.5 Reach the oasis and valley beyond.

Fortynine Palms Oasis

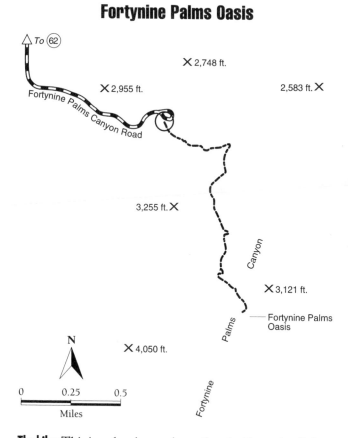

The hike: This is a clear but rocky trail to the Fortynine Palms Oasis. From the parking lot it climbs to its highest point in the first half of the trip. From this elevation you have a view of Twentynine Palms, and shortly thereafter, as the trail curves to the right at 0.3 mile, you have your first glimpse of the palms, down in a rocky gorge 0.75 mile ahead. The descent to the oasis traverses dry, rocky terrain; even the desert shrubs are dwarfed by the harsh conditions. Miniature barrel cacti dot the slopes. The windy dry hills above make the oasis even more striking.

At Fortynine Palms Oasis (1.5 miles), the huge old palms tower above a dense willow thicket that provides a congenial habitat for numerous desert birds. Hummingbirds are frequent visitors. The canyon is also a mecca for the desert bighorn sheep. In this idyllic setting, the palm trees have a bizarre appearance. Their fire-scarred trunks bear tragic witness to the destructive urges of knife-wielding visitors who have tattooed the trunks with initials, signs, and names. The sight of these assaults on the palms is incongruous in such a setting and is highly disturbing. But the fire that caused the blackened trunks, whether caused by lightning or careless humans, may actually benefit the fire-resistant palm trees by clearing out competing vegetation, such as mesquite and arrowweed. The lushness of the oasis is all the more appealing given the starkness of its surroundings.

Option: For the adventurous and energetic explorer, the canyon beyond the oasis (to the right) can be explored for as long as time and interest permit. The use trail is intermittent and the boulders are challenging, but the curving canyon is inviting. After your exploration, the hike back to the parking lot provides sweeping views of the desert below.

Note: Day use only is permitted in this area to protect bighorn sheep's access to water.

19
INDIAN COVE NATURE TRAIL

Highlights: A nature trail featuring wash vegetation.
Type of hike: Loop.
Total distance: 0.6 mile.
Elevation gain: Minimal.
Best months: October–April.
Maps: Trails Illustrated Joshua Tree National Park Map; USGS Indian Cove quad.
Parking and trailhead facilities: The campground and signed parking area are next to the trailhead.

Finding the trailhead: Go 9.8 miles east of Park Boulevard in Joshua Tree on California 62, then take Indian Cove Road south for 3 miles to Indian Cove Campground. Bear right at the Y intersection, and follow the signs for the nature trail parking area. From the east, take CA 62 for 7 miles west of the Utah Trail intersection in Twentynine Palms; take Indian Cove Road south for 3 miles to the campground and follow signs to the parking lot for the nature trail.

Key points:
0.0 Trailhead.
0.2 Exit the wash.
0.6 Reach the end of the loop.

Indian Cove Nature Trail

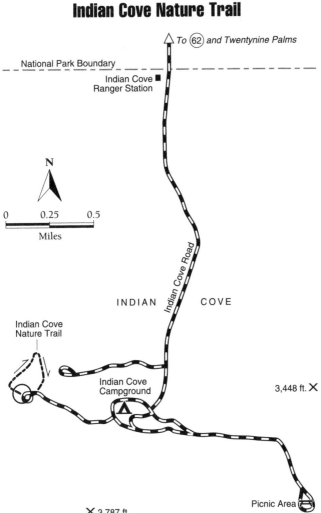

To (62) and Twentynine Palms

National Park Boundary

Indian Cove
Ranger Station

N

0   0.25   0.5
Miles

Indian Cove
Nature Trail

INDIAN   COVE

Indian Cove Road

Indian Cove
Campground

3,448 ft. ✕

✕ 3,787 ft.

Picnic Area

The hike: This interpretive nature trail is one of the more difficult ones to follow due to the scarcity of arrows, trail indicators, and informational signs. The trail skirts alongside boulders at the north end of Wonderland of Rocks. It begins just west of the parking area, travels across an alluvial fan, and goes down into a broad wash. A short 0.2 mile later, it exits the wash and returns to the parking area.

The information provided ranges from background on Paleo-Indians, to desert plant and animal identification, to physical geology. There is no thematic common denominator.

It is easy to miss the path's exit from the wash. Watch for the identification sign for the desert senna on your right immediately after the paperbag bush sign. That is your signal to bear right out of the wash to pick up the trail back to the parking area.

Wall Street Mill, Wonderland Wash, Barker Dam Nature Trail, and Hidden Valley Nature Trail

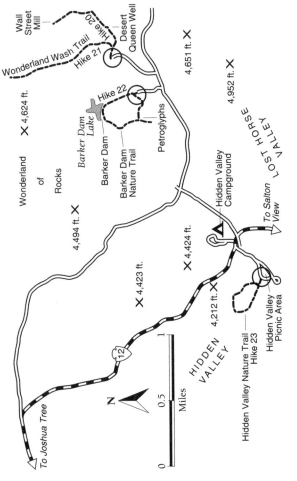

Wall Street Mill

Wonderland Wash Trail Hike 21

Hike 20

Desert Queen Well

Wonderland of Rocks

X 4,624 ft.

X 4,494 ft.

Hike 22

Barker Dam Lake

Barker Dam

Barker Dam Nature Trail

Petroglyphs

4,651 ft. X

4,952 ft. X

LOST HORSE VALLEY

Hidden Valley Campground

To Salton View

X 4,423 ft.

X 4,424 ft.

4,212 ft. X

Hidden Valley Picnic Area

Hidden Valley Nature Trail Hike 23

HIDDEN VALLEY

12

To Joshua Tree

N

Miles

0   0.5   1

20
WALL STREET MILL

Highlights: A historic, well-preserved ore processing mill and other remnants of early mining days.
Type of hike: Out-and-back.
Total distance: 1.5 miles.
Elevation gain: Minimal.
Best months: October–April.
Maps: Trails Illustrated Joshua Tree National Park Map; USGS Indian Cove quad.
Parking and trailhead facilities: There is an unsigned parking area, a portable toilet, and a bike rack at the end of the dirt road.

Finding the trailhead: From California 62 in Joshua Tree, take the Park Boulevard exit and drive 1 mile south to where it becomes Quail Springs Road. Continue on Quail Springs Road for 4 miles to the park's west entrance. Follow Park Route 12 southeast for 8.7 miles to Hidden Valley Campground/Barker Dam Road. Turn left (east) into the campground. Bear right immediately after the entrance and follow the dirt road for 1.6 miles to Barker Dam Road. Continue beyond the Barker Dam turnoff for 0.15 mile to the next dirt road to your left (north). The sign at the turn reads "Day Use Only/Area Closed 6 P.M. to 6 A.M." The parking area is 0.25 mile from the sign.

Key points:

0.0 Trailhead. At the fork at 25 yards, follow the trail to the right. The ruins of a pink adobe ranch house are 200 yards to your left.

0.1 Two trails converge; a rusty old truck is 50 yards to your left. If you investigate the pink house ruins to the left, you will rejoin the Mill route here.

0.2 The windmill and debris are on your right; continue north, parallel to Wonderland.

0.4 Reach the monument commemorating the death of Bagley.

0.6 The two-track drops into the wash and becomes more trail-like.

0.7 A park sign reading "Preserve America's Past" appears among the oak trees; the mill site and various vehicles are on your left.

The hike: This level hike displays the desert's power of preservation! Rusty old trucks still have their tires. Antique cars sit peacefully beneath oak trees. The mill, protected by the National Register of Historic Sites due to its local technological and mechanical uniqueness, still stands with its machinery intact, albeit a tad rusty. A barbed wire fence also protects the mill from visitors. Nearby are hulks of vehicles and other artifacts of life in the desert from 60 years ago. A park sign at the mill explains its workings, with an excellent drawing—actually a blueprint of its original design in the 1930s. This is a fun voyage of discovery, even for those who might not be machinery buffs.

The ranch house to the left of the trail near the trailhead and the windmill at 0.2 mile are remnants of the ranching era in the Queen Valley. The Keys family has been involved in both ranching and mining and still has a private inholding, the Desert Queen Ranch, to the west of this trail.

The Wall Street Mill was part of the Keys' industrial complex. Built by Bill Keys to process the ore from the Desert Queen Mine, it was in operation for only a few years before falling into disuse. One reason for its short life span is that Bill Keys had a run-in with Worth Bagley, his neighbor, over the use of the road to the mill. The painted rock at 0.4 mile marks the spot of the final altercation and of Bagley's death. Convicted of murder, Keys spent 5 years in San Quentin, but was later exonerated. Apparently he had shot Bagley in self-defense.

The Wall Street Mill is at 0.75 mile. Return to the parking area by the same wash/trail.

The trail shares its trailhead with the Wonderland Wash hike (Hike 21). The proximity of the mill and the mounds of monzogranite provide an appropriate contrast between the reign of humans and of nature in this wild country.

21
WONDERLAND WASH

see map page 70

Highlights: Spectacular rock formations of all shapes and sizes, in every direction.
Type of hike: Out-and-back.
Total distance: 2 miles.
Elevation gain: Minimal.
Best months: September–May.
Maps: Trails Illustrated Joshua Tree National Park Map; USGS Indian Cove quad.
Parking and trailhead facilities: The unsigned trailhead is on a dirt road with a parking area, portable toilet, and bike rack.

Finding the trailhead: From California 62 in the town of Joshua Tree, take Park Boulevard south for 1 mile to where it becomes Quail Springs Road. Continue on Quail Springs Road for 4 miles to the park's west entrance. Continue southeast on Park Route 12 for 8.7 miles to Hidden Valley Campground. Turn left (east) into the campground, and take the immediate right turn (signed to Barker Dam). Follow the dirt road 1.7 miles to the first road on your left after the signed Barker Dam turnoff. The only sign on Wonderland Wash road is "Day Use Only/Area Closed 6 P.M. to 6 A.M." Drive north 0.25 mile to a large unsigned parking area, which is also the trailhead for the Wall Street Mill hike (Hike 20).

Key points:
0.0 At the first fork immediately beyond the trailhead, bear left to the ruins of a pink adobe ranch house.
0.3 Cut by the house and enter the wash to your left.
1.0 Reach the Astro Domes—huge domes of monzogranite.

The hike: The use trail into Wonderland Wash is easy to follow due to the footsteps of the hundreds of rock climbers who enjoy the acres of grainy mounds of White Tank granite. From the parking area, follow the trail to the first fork, and bear left toward the ruins of a pink house, which you can see from the fork. Head for the house and follow the beaten path to the left into the nearby shallow wash at 0.3 mile, only about 50 feet from the house site. The narrow wash is easy to follow, with periodic pathways weaving from bank to bank as you follow it northward into the Wonderland.

Plentiful oak and prickly pear, as well as the remnants of a dam in the wash, are other attractions of this hike—but the primary focus is on the huge rock formations stretching in all directions in an enchanted world of whimsically eroded granite mounds. Well into the wash (1 mile from the trailhead) are the formations known to rock climbers who enjoy scaling their massive surfaces as the Astro Domes. You can usually hear climbers' voices echoing from various points among the boulders, and their silhouettes may startle you when they appear hundreds of feet above, atop these obelisks.

The return trip down the wash to the trailhead is equally interesting, providing views of the rock formations from a different perspective.

22
BARKER DAM NATURE TRAIL

see map page 70

Highlights: A nature trail, the only lake in the park, and an archaeological site.
Type of hike: Loop.
Total distance: 1.1 mile.
Elevation gain: Minimal.
Best months: October–May.
Maps: Trails Illustrated Joshua Tree National Park Map; USGS Indian Cove quad.
Parking and trailhead facilities: There is a signed parking lot at the trailhead.

Finding the trailhead: From California 62 in Joshua Tree, take Park Boulevard south for 1 mile to where it turns into Quail Springs Road. Continue on Quail Springs Road for 4 miles to the park's west entrance. Follow Park Route 12 for 8.7 miles to Hidden Valley Campground and the Barker Dam turnoff to the left (east); bear right at the signed road immediately after entering the campground and drive 1.6 miles to the Barker Dam parking lot.

Key points:
0.0 Barker Dam Nature Trail trailhead.
0.4 Arrive at Barker Dam Lake.
0.8 Reach the petroglyphs.
1.1 Arrive at the end of the loop at the parking lot.

The hike: This hike provides easy access to the Wonderland of Rocks, the only lake in the park, and to a rich array of petroglyphs. The Wonderland of Rocks is a jumbled maze of nearly 8,000 acres of granite interspersed with Joshua trees. The Barker Dam area is open to visitors only between 8 A.M. and 6 P.M. so bighorn sheep can find water without human disturbance.

The highly informative nature trail is a step back in time, both in terms of prehistory and with respect to futile, short-lived attempts to raise cattle back in the early 1900s. Barker Dam was built by ranchers Barker and Shay in a natural rock catch basin to store water for cattle. In 1949 and 1950, the dam was raised by Bill Keys, owner of the Desert Queen Mine and the nearby Desert Queen Ranch, still a private inholding. When filled to capacity by seasonal rains, the lake behind the dam encompasses 20 acres. Because it is surrounded by a magnificent rock ring of monzonite granite, it looks almost as though it is nestled in a high Sierra cirque at 11,000 feet. Today, the lake is used by bighorn sheep and many other species of wildlife, including shorebirds and migratory waterfowl—some of the last creatures you would expect to find in the desert!

The trail is clear and sandy, winding through a couple of tight places in the rocks, reaching Barker Dam at 0.4 mile. Notable plant species en route include turbinella oak, adapted to the high Mojave Desert above 4,000 feet, and nolina—a yucca look-alike that provided food for the Cahuilla Indians, who baked it like molasses.

Below the dam are interesting manmade stone structures. Here, the innovative Bill Keys built stone watering basins designed to prevent spillage of the precious desert water. It could be said that water is more precious than gold here; Keys was involved with both commodities.

From Barker Dam Lake, the trail heads west and south through a series of intimate little alcove-like valleys containing rock-lined gardens of Joshua trees, cholla cacti, and yucca. At 0.8 mile the trail reaches a signed path leading 100 feet right to a large panel of petroglyphs, early Native American stone etchings. The petroglyphs are on the face of a large rock amphitheater and overhang. Sadly, a movie crew once painted the carvings so they would show up better on film. The rock faces just to the southeast of these vandalized petroglyphs contain undamaged petroglyphs that are largely concealed by dense brush. This early encampment of immeasurable value includes rock mortars used for grinding nuts and seeds, along with petroglyphs of a scorpion, a man with long fingers, women with dresses who were likely early settlers, and other figures better left to your imagination. Vegetation is being reestablished along this cliff wall, so please be careful to avoid trampling the new plantings and other vegetation.

The loop continues another 0.3 mile back to the parking area and trailhead.

23
HIDDEN VALLEY NATURE TRAIL

see map page 70

Highlights: A valley surrounded by mounds of monzogranite.
Type of hike: Loop.
Total distance: 1 mile.
Elevation gain: Minimal.
Best months: October–April.
Maps: Trails Illustrated Joshua Tree National Park Map; USGS Indian Cove quad.
Parking and trailhead facilities: There is a signed nature trail, parking, and a picnic area at the trailhead.

Finding the trailhead: From California 62 at Joshua Tree, take the Park Boulevard exit south for 1 mile to where it becomes Quail Springs Road. Continue on Quail Springs Road for 4.3 miles to the park's west entrance; stay on the same road (now Park Route 12) for 8.7 miles to Hidden Valley Nature Trail and Picnic Area, which is on your right (south). After you turn off the main road, follow the dirt road to the right for less than 0.1 mile to the parking area.

Key points:
0.0 From the parking area, the trail goes into the narrow canyon leading to the valley.
0.1 At the junction, follow the trail left around the valley.
1.0 Reach the end of the loop.

The hike: This interpretive trail emphasizes the area's historical uses as it travels the 1-mile perimeter of Hidden Valley with very little change in elevation. The setting is a snug valley surrounded by massive granite formations.

The trail from the parking area winds upward through the boulders to the hidden valley. This part of the trail consists of old asphalt, so following it is easy. The rest of the journey is unpaved, but is clearly marked with signs, arrows, or fallen logs. A bit of the entry trail requires negotiating around and over moderate boulders, but a bright new wooden bridge takes you over the most challenging part.

Many possible pathways diverge in all directions within the level valley. Most are created by the numerous rock climbers who are attracted to the massive blocks of granite that create the valley walls. It is likely you will hear climbers' shouts echoing off the rocks and spot these adventuresome park visitors dangling on ropes or standing on top of the immense boulders.

To follow the historical signs in chronological order, go left when you enter the valley, 0.1 mile from the trailhead.

Indian life and settlers' activities are the emphasis in the early part of the trail. The abnormally high rainfall (10 inches per year) of the late nineteenth century led to the development of cattle ranching. The McHaney Gang allegedly used Hidden Valley as a base camp for their large rustling operation in the southwest, until they turned their energies to gold mining. They began developing the Desert Queen Mine in 1895. It was eventually taken over by Bill Keys, who became quite the desert magnate—a successful rancher and miner—until his death in 1969.

The advent of the automobile in the 1920s brought new visitors aplenty to the desert, seriously endangering the fragile environment. In the 1930s, Minerva Hamilton Hoyt led efforts to protect the region, resulting finally in Franklin D. Roosevelt's 1936 establishment of Joshua Tree National Monument. In 1950, the monument's size was reduced in order to permit extensive mining. The larger area was restored with the California Desert Protection Act of 1994, when the area was designated a national park. The nature trail provides a thorough overview of this history, as well as a parting reminder to the visitor to remain vigilant as a protector of our desert resources.

Note: This is a day-use area; no camping is permitted.

High View Nature Trail
South Park Peak

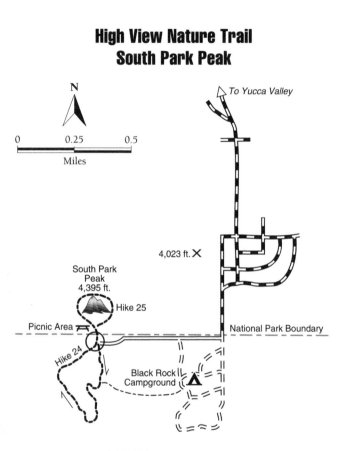

24
HIGH VIEW NATURE TRAIL

Highlights: A peak hike with panoramic views of the park's western section.
Type of hike: Loop.
Total distance: 1.3 miles.
Elevation gain: 320 feet.
Best months: October–May.
Maps: Trails Illustrated Joshua Tree National Park Map; USGS Yucca Valley South quad.
Parking and trailhead facilities: The signed parking area is adjacent to a dirt road.

Finding the trailhead: From California 62 in Yucca Valley, turn south on Avalon Avenue and drive 0.7 mile to where it becomes Palomar Avenue. Continue on Palomar Avenue for 2.3 miles and turn left on Joshua Lane. Take Joshua Lane for 1 mile to a T intersection at San Marino Drive. Turn right and go 0.3 mile to Black Rock Road. Turn left on Black Rock Road and drive south 0.5 mile to the park's entrance. Immediately before the entrance, turn right (west) onto a dirt road and go west 0.8 mile to the parking area.

Key points:
0.0 Trailhead.
0.8 Reach the summit.

The hike: This nature trail travels to the top of a hill, providing a view over the Yucca Valley and the northern reaches of the park. There is a register at the summit at 0.8 mile, as well as a bench. The 1.3-mile long trail follows a relatively gentle route as it climbs 320 feet. Numbered sites line the trail; brochures are available at the Black Rock ranger station in the adjacent campground.

Option: If you're staying at the nearby Black Rock Campground, a hilly but very scenic route connects the campground with the nature trail. It leaves from the top of the loop above the ranger station and enters the nature loop in its first section. Although clearly marked, this alternate route to the campground has an aura of wilderness. On our loop hike from the campground, we spotted two coyotes hunting for rabbits in the middle of the afternoon.

25
SOUTH PARK PEAK

see map page 82

Highlights: Sweeping vistas of the northwestern section of the park.
Type of hike: Loop.
Total distance: 0.8 mile.
Elevation gain: 250 feet.
Best months: October–April
Maps: Trails Illustrated Joshua Tree National Park Map; USGS Yucca Valley South quad.
Parking and trailhead facilities: There is a parking area near the end of a dirt road.

Finding the trailhead: From California 62 in Yucca Valley, take Avalon Avenue south for 0.7 mile to where it becomes Palomar Avenue. Continue on Palomar Avenue for 2.3 miles to Joshua Lane. Turn left onto Joshua Lane and drive 1 mile to the T intersection with San Marino Drive. Turn right on San Marino Drive and go 0.3 mile to its end at Black Rock Road. Turn left on Black Rock Road, and go 0.5 mile to the park entrance. Immediately before the entrance, turn right (west) on the dirt road. Follow it for 0.8 mile to the parking area. The unsigned trail to the peak begins at the northwest corner of the parking area.

Key points:
0.0 South Park Peak Trailhead.
0.2 Reach a park bench.
0.4 Arrive on the summit of South Park Peak.

The hike: Although this short loop hike lies just outside Joshua Tree National Park's northern boundary, it provides a sweeping view of the park's northwestern section and the town of Joshua Tree in the valley below. This gentle peak climb begins as an easy dirt trail. At 0.2 mile there is a comfortable bench where you can enjoy the excellent view. Another bench adorns the summit at 0.4 mile. The trail between the benches is steeper and rockier than the section from the parking area.

The peak boasts quite a register. With a concrete pedestal and a Plexiglas box, it is an impressive item. The stack of registers within the box makes great reading while you are resting on the bench. Lots of literary visitors climb South Peak.

Yucca Valley's sprawl and its subdivisions closing in on the park are swirling on the north—while to the south lies the vast space of Joshua Tree National Park. As many that signed the register noted, this sight is confirmation that national park status is the best protection for desert areas, particularly near expanding population centers.

Follow the trail past the register box for the descent to the wash on the backside of the peak and the walk back to the parking area.

About the Authors

Polly Burke and Bill Cunningham are partners on the long trail of Life. Polly, formerly a history teacher in St. Louis, Missouri, now makes her home with Bill in Choteau, Montana. She is pursuing multiple careers in freelance writing, leading wilderness group trips, and working with the developmentally disabled. Polly has hiked and backpacked extensively throughout many parts of the country.

Bill is a lifelong "wildernut," as a conservation activist, backpacking outfitter, and field studies teacher for the University of Montana. During the 1970s and 1980s he was a field representative for The Wilderness Society. He has written several books and dozens of magazine articles about wilderness areas based on extensive on-the-ground knowledge. He is the author of *Wild Montana*, the first in Falcon Publishing's series of guidebooks to wilderness and unprotected roadless areas.

Polly and Bill coauthored Falcon's *Hiking California's Desert Parks* (1996), *Wild Utah* (1998), and *Hiking the Gila Wilderness* (1999). Writing about the vast desert expanses of Joshua Tree has been especially rewarding because long ago the authors both lived in California close to the desert—Bill in Bakersfield and Polly in San Diego. They have especially enjoyed renewing their ties to California while exploring the state's desert regions. They want others to have as much fun exploring the desert as they did.